HENRI ROUSSEAU

Title page: SELF-PORTRAIT WITH OIL LAMP, 1902-1903
Oil on canvas, 9″ × 7″ (23 × 19 cm)
Musée Picasso, Paris

Series published under the direction of:
MADELEINE LEDIVELEC-GLOECKNER

Translation from the French:
S. M. ROUVE

Library of Congress Cataloging in Publication Data

Vallier, Dora.
  [Henri Rousseau. English]
  Henri Rousseau / Dora Vallier.
  p. cm. — (Crown art library)
  Translated from the French.
  Includes bibliographical references.
  ISBN 0-517-53697-8: $ 14.95
  1. Rousseau, Henri Julien Félix, 1844-1910 — Criticism and
interpretation. 2. Primitivism in art — France. I. Rousseau, Henri
Julien Félix, 1844-1910. II. Title. III. Series.
ND553.R67V33   1991   90-55847
759.4 — dc20   CIP

Henri Rousseau

by Dora Vallier

CROWN PUBLISHERS, INC. - NEW YORK

Henri Rousseau, the Douanier

a file

Right at the start, it is only fair to stress that the entire work of the Douanier Rousseau slips through the net cast by our comments on art, makes irrelevant the precautions which we are wont to take, blocks all usual approaches, defies all classifications — in a word challenges the esthetic raster of art history. Any attempt to measure Rousseau's activity against that raster would be to no avail and would only prove that we are dealing with an artist who eludes our grasp. This is why we have chosen to set up a file on Rousseau, juxtaposing biography and art, eliciting the strangeness that inextricably intertwines them and, finally, isolating the insoluble contradictions that are there.

The years in which Rousseau appeared on the scene, that dazzling second half of the nineteenth century, witness the great schism in art: on the one side, there is the respect for the authority of the past, upheld by the academies; on the other, its transgression in the name of modernity. But, for Rousseau, there is no place whatsoever in this division — and this is only too obvious. Academic painting rests on received knowledge consecrated by tradition. Such painting begins with technical apprenticeship which in itself is a work-model, all the more compulsive because it is part and parcel of the actual ways of art. Reiterating well-tried devices, academic pictures end in a preordained pattern of perception. They transmit already-known messages. And they end by displaying an utter lack of authenticity which the customs-officer-turned-painter could not attain at all, since he lacked the necessary culture, education and technical know-how. But therein lay a fascination which would haunt him all his life. Yet at the same time and for the same reasons, lack of culture, education and know-how, he could not join the ranks of the transgressors of academic precepts. Impressionism, Neo-Impressionism, Fauvism and Cubism, which unfolded during his lifetime, simply did not exist for him. However, the transgression embodied in his own painting is much more far-reaching than the ways and means of those innovative artists who would bring about the concept of avant-garde. The fact is that their transgression was rationally worked out. Rousseau's violation, on the other hand, surged from the deepest recesses of the subconscious and, what is more, never ceased to be handicapped by his obsessive wish to be the peer of the academic artists. Hence the powerful tension in all his pictures, as if he were the living embodiment of the rift between avant-garde and academicism that bore the mark of his time. Hence also the thorough break which he inflicted on art history in forcefully exploding its conventional patterns.

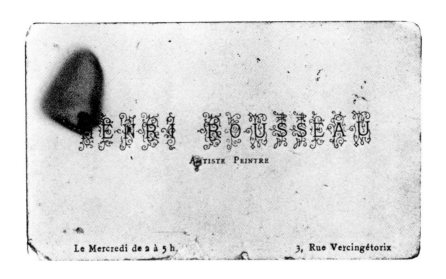

Henri Rousseau, the artist

«Born at Laval in 1844, he was obliged at first, in view of his parents' lack of means, to follow a career different from that to which his artistic tastes called him.

Therefore it was not until 1885 that he made his debut in Art after many disappointments, alone and without any master but nature and some advice from Gérôme and Clément. His first two creations exhibited were sent to the Salon des Champs-Elysées and were entitled *Italian Dance* and *Sunset*.

The following year he painted *Carnival Evening* and *Thunderclap*. And then, *Waiting, A Poor Devil, After the Banquet, Departure, Dinner on the Grass, Suicide, To My Father, Myself. Portrait-Landscape of the Author, Tiger Pursuing Explorers, The Centenary of Independence, Liberty, Last of the 51ˢᵗ, War, Portrait-Genre of the Writer A. J.,* about two hundred pen-and-pencil drawings, and a number of landscapes of Paris and environs.

It is only after very great hardships that he succeeded in making himself known to the numerous artists now around him. He has improved himself more and more in the original style adopted by him and he is in the process of becoming one of our best realist painters. As a distinctive feature, he sports a bushy beard and has long been a member of the Indépendants, convinced that any pioneer whose thoughts aspire to the beautiful and the good should be permitted to create in complete freedom.

He will never forget the members of the press who have been able to understand him and have supported him in his moments of discouragement, and who will have helped to make him what he must become.

Done at Paris, July 10, 1895»

Portrait of the Artist, 1895. Pen drawing. Collection: Santa-Marina, Buenos Aires

All through this autobiographical sketch «he» replaces «I». Rousseau wrote it with a definite goal in mind: the publisher and printer Girard-Coutances, having already put on the market a certain number of biographies of contemporary writers under the ambitious title «Portraits of the Next Century,» had announced a second volume dealing with painters and sculptors. It was then that Rousseau set about writing his autobiography and sent it, unsolicited, to the publisher together with a pen-drawn self-portrait. But this second volume was never published. All that remains of this project (from which, it goes without saying, Rousseau had been omitted in advance) is this brief text, which seems quite banal at first sight but which, when scrutinized at close quarters, turns out to be a rather exceptional document. Compelled by circumstances to talk about himself in the third person, Rousseau

Photograph of Rousseau as a young man

had to step back and project himself on to his life and work, presenting himself more truly than anyone else could have done by the written word. Utterly neutral terms build up the most personal of all portraits. Indifferent utterances are transmuted into confessions. All is said, through Rousseau's most intimate thought which sneaks into this anodyne, almost trivial sentence: «is in the process of becoming one of our best realist painters.» At that time he must have been the only one to think so. This statement, extremely subjective when it was formulated, pierces the deliberate objectivity of Rousseau's words and yet leads us into a mirror-maze, because today nothing could be more objective than the verdict that Rousseau was one of the greatest painters of the last century. Subjective, objective: where does the one begin and the other end? I, he: I/mirror-maze within which we shall proceed to read Rousseau's autobiographical sketch, sentence by sentence.

All through the nineteenth century, having perhaps benefited from a sale of public properties, the Rousseau family lived in Beucheresse Gate, a remnant of Laval's fortified wall, at the heart of the old town, at the foot of the castle. Before her marriage, Rousseau's mother had lived in the Rue des Serruriers, a narrow alley at the back of Beucheresse Gate: a world of nearby horizons revealed by the local Registry of births, marriages and deaths. Julien Rousseau was by trade a tinker, as his father, Julien-Gervais, had been before him. His son Henri was also named Julien, and occasionally he signed Henri Julien Rousseau. But with him the family tradition comes to an end.

In 1947, in a letter to the Mayor of Laval, Rousseau's granddaughter, who had only very rarely met her grandfather during some holidays, recalled the memories of her mother, who had lived with him only until she was twelve, and declared: « In our family, artist was synonymous with perdition. »

The family never owned any of his paintings, not a single one, either during his lifetime or after his death. And after his death, as his daughter was about to clear his lodgings, Robert Delaunay arrived, unfortunately too late to rescue the drawings which she had already torn to pieces and thrown away. All he managed to save from destruction were the notebooks on which Rousseau, throughout his career, had pasted pressclippings about himself, often in duplicate in order to give greater bulk to the volume to which, especially at the beginning, he kept adding handwritten marginal comments.

Because of his father's debts, the house in which Rousseau was born was legally seized when he was only seven. His family having left town, he became a boarder at Laval High School, which he had been attending as a day student. A mediocre student, he was nevertheless awarded a couple of prizes, one for vocal music and the other for drawing. These distinctions have been recorded in his biographies because not only is he a world-famous artist, but he is also the author of a forgotten waltz bearing the name of his first wife, Clémence. He was fifteen when he married her in Paris in 1859. A bailiff's clerk in the early days of his marriage, a few months later he had found a position with the city's toll authority. This checking of goods at the Paris gates, an invariable and intermittent chore, work in the margin of work, left intact the inner freedom of the man engaged in it. This was Rousseau's stroke of luck.

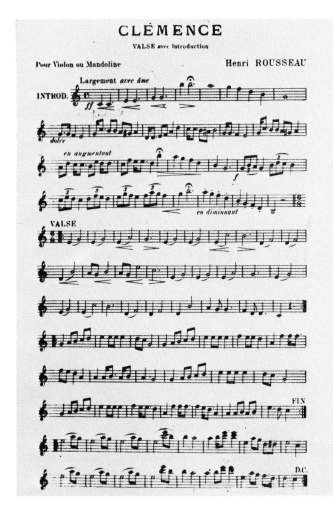

Two clumsy drawings and an astonishing small picture are the only witnesses of the long years during which, day in day out, Rousseau worked for the Paris Customs, at the river toll on the Auteuil Embankment and also at Vanves Gate. This was one of the gates in the city wall widened in the reign of Louis XVI, and where barriers halted vehicles and travelers, allowing into town only merchandise and foodstuffs for which the statutory duty had been paid. At that farthest edge of the town, his eyes wandering over the suburbs that had attracted him all his life, Rousseau yielded to his artistic tastes. Pencil in hand, he observed his surroundings and assiduously endeavoured to reproduce them. Clumsily he learned to draw using the pages of a pocket-size notebook. In one of these drawings, his attention was focused on a tree. In those never-changing days at the tollgate there must have been in sight some tree on which he learned to follow the passing of light, the ripple of the wind, the rotation of seasons. Could it be that he became a painter because he so loved trees? The image of a tree as a matrix of his art: this may well have been his fate. A description of Laval by the town clerk Trohel may then be worth recalling: « The new east districts sprawl over flat country, a bluish tide of roofs from which emerge the slender shapes of bell towers ... and trees, trees, and yet more trees ... »

This was the prime element in Rousseau's painting, the mainspring of his entire evolution. The more he gave free rein to his deep self, the more the vegetal structures grew relevant; the more he asserted himself, the more they proliferated in his canvases to become finally the burgeoning virgin forests. And this flourishing verdure recalls the same matrix, the same initial tree.

« My superiors at the tollgate used to assign me to less demanding duties so that I would find it easier to work. » But did they go as far as to allow him to set up his easel in his workplace? It hardly seems probable. The extraordinary painting known as *The Tollgate* is therefore through and through the work of a Sunday painter endowed with an unheard-of color sense. He started from a dominant: green, and this green, by irresistibly attracting everything, ended by transfiguring the gloomy townscape (recorded in a photograph) into a rural site. A lawn takes the place of the paving stones. Trees blossom out. Not only had the subject changed, but the entire composition had been worked out on the basis of the green and in function of its nuances. The transitions from one green to another graded the planes from darkest to lightest to reach the yellow on the edges of the leaves at the very back of the canvas. Alternatively, two different greens, one faintly more tinged with blue than the other, mark in the foreground the lawn divided by a road. These chromatic details, to which are to be added others such as the tiny dark blue cart near the black fence, testify beyond any shadow of a doubt that Rousseau was most sensitive to the color-subduing presence of air. To put it differently, he grasped the effect of distance on colors. He never managed to understand the functioning of linear perspective, which is but a complement to, and a refinement of, the rendering of three-dimensional space. Because of this constant discrepancy, he inserted into his paintings the irreducible difference between a linguistic convention (linear perspective) and an immediate grasp of the sensitivity (aerial perspective) which coexist within the figurative tradition of the Renaissance. And in this, he is truly unique.

Quai d'Auteuil, 1885
Ink drawing, 6¼″ × 3⅞″ (16 × 10 cm)
Ex-collection of Max Weber

Quai d'Auteuil, 1885
Ink drawing, 5¾″ × 4⅜″ (14.5 × 11 cm)
Ex-collection of Max Weber

13

These four pictures, which treat the san.
painting from beginning to end. They rev
becomes unreal in the midst of a space

Carnival Evening, 1886
Oil on canvas, 45⅝″ × 35″ (116 × 89 cm)
Philadelphia Museum of Art. Collection Louis E. Stern

Walk in the Forest, between, 1886–90
Oil on canvas, 27⅞″ × 23¾″ (71 × 60 cm)
Kunsthaus, Zurich

ect, show the development of Rousseau's
increasing importance of plant life, which
ived in an ever more irrational manner.

Woman Walking in a Tropical Forest, 1905
Oil on canvas, 39⅜" × 31⅞" (100 × 81 cm)
Barnes Foundation, Merion, Pennsylvania

Woman in Red in the Forest, 1905–10
Oil on canvas, 29½" × 23¼" (75 × 59 cm)
Ex-collection Paul Guillaume

The Toll House at the Porte de Vanves, in Rousseau's Time
Photograph by Adget, Musée Carnavalet, Paris

L'Octroi (The Toll House), 1890. Oil on canvas, 15⅝″ × 12⅞″ (37.5 × 32.5 cm)
Courtauld Institute of Art, University of London

THE PROMENADE, 1886–90. Oil on canvas, 18⅛″ × 21⅝″ (46 × 55 cm). Private collection, Basel

THE FISHERMAN, 1909. Oil on canvas, 15″ × 18⅛″ (38 × 46 cm). Collection: Michael Bakwin

What does it mean to make a first appearance in art when one is toiling at a Paris tollgate, when one's family are victims of tuberculosis, that nineteenth-century scourge of a certain social class? Seven out of his nine children had died at an early age. (Late in life, he had even lost track of these ordeals.) His wife too had died in 1888. After more than twenty years of employment, he was entitled to an early retirement, and he made up his mind: in 1893, at the age of forty-nine, the tollgate attendant Henri Julien Rousseau left his employment. Posterity has awarded him the honorific rank of Customs Inspector (« Douanier »), to which his much humbler station in life gave him no right.

That same year Rousseau became a full-time painter. But in his own mind he had considered himself a full-fledged artist ever since the first showing of his work in public. That is why he gave 1885 as the date of his « first appearance.» In his eyes, exhibiting at the Salon des Indépendants was sufficient to confer on him the status of artist. And in a way he was right, though he did not know it. There is no doubt that, had Rousseau lived before the foundation of the Salon des Indépendants, we would not even have heard of him, for the simple reason that artistic life, centered on the Salon des Artistes Français with its decrepit academic offerings, would have excluded, on principle and forever, such an autodidact. But he never realized this predicament. The revolutionary aspect of a salon without a jury, such as the Indépendants which showed his works for twenty-five years and carved for him a place in history, remained utterly beyond his comprehension, as did also the decline of academic tradition denounced by the founding members of the Indépendants. Loyal to their salon, he nonetheless idolized Gérôme.

If this was so, what could have been the hopes blighted before his beginnings? Does he hint at technical failures in his work or at some thwarted attempt to be admitted to the Salon des Artistes Français? No one will ever know, because for this tollgate attendant whom art had captured the words « first appearance » are ambivalent. Not only do they denote an inward initiation, but they also suggest an outward meaning: « I exhibit, therefore I am an artist. »

MEADOW, BANKS OF THE OISE, 1907
Oil on canvas, 12¼″ × 19⅝″ (21.5 × 35.5 cm)
Fogg Art Museum, Harvard University, Cambridge, Massachusetts

THE SAWMILL, OUTSKIRTS OF PARIS, 1890–93
Oil on canvas, 10″ × 17¾″ (24.5 × 45.5 cm)
The Art Institute of Chicago. Bequest of Kate L. Brewster

Rousseau to Arsène Alexandre:

> Nothing makes me happier than to contemplate nature and to paint it. Would you believe it that when I go out in the country and see all that sun, all that greenery and all those flowers, I sometimes say to myself: All that belongs to me, it does!

Apollinaire:

> As soon as the weather would clear, he would wander in the woods around Paris to gather a profusion of leaves which he would then copy.

Rousseau again:

> Talking of landscapes, I draw small sketches from nature, but I always rework them on a bigger scale in the studio.

When Monet had dragged his fellow students at the Beaux-Arts, Renoir and Sisley, out to work in the open air in the Fontainebleau Forest, his had been an act of revolt against academic education. It laid the foundation for a new visual system that was to overthrow the prevailing monolithic concept of art dictated by the Academy and to impose a direct vision of reality. Rousseau took the same stand in all innocence. For him it was the unavoidable consequence of his exaltation in front of nature, coupled with the desire to make it his own: « All that belongs to me, it does. » To capture a wild animal, did prehistoric man not trace its outline on cave walls? Art as prey — and art as institution.

Rousseau strove to bring them together. A painter with no formal knowledge of history, he clung to history which for him was embodied in official art, whose obsolescence he failed to see. To the desire to make nature his own, he added the will to imitate a clearly defined technique. But as he had not been instructed in these techniques, he painted in search of equivalences. Parallel to, but distinct from, his initial recourse to splintered and close brushstrokes, another technique emerged after 1880: wide flat strokes corresponding, in his mind, to academic textures. This was the limit that his improvised acquaintance with pictorial devices enabled him to reach. But academic texture was achieved through the chiaroscuro and the profusion of glazes that enhance the relief of the figures. It is therefore the very denial of any flat coloring. What followed is yet another paradox: anxious to imitate a technique of the past, Rousseau was catapulted into the future. He painted as artists would in the twentieth century, after Matisse.

Pen drawing. Ex-collection of H. von Garvens, Hanover

Pencil drawing

An intriguing inversion has taken place in the statement in which Rousseau suggested a tutor/pupil relationship, mentioning Gérôme and Clément. This obscure self-taught painter moves from century to century in a blaze of light while these academic celebrities who left him awestruck have sunk into oblivion, so much so that, in referring to his work, we practically have to unearth them. If their canvases had not been so scattered, not to say lost, buried in museum storerooms, and hardly known because in their time reproductions were few and far between, then it is certain that a study of them would enable us to better understand Rousseau's ambitions. Linking Gérôme and Clément to his apprenticeship was a device to confer upon himself artistic credentials to which he knew he was not entitled. He insisted on mentioning these two artists any time his biography was discussed. Toward the end of his life, he also added the name of Bonnat. This was not a matter of mere chance. Each one of these three famous academic painters had indeed mattered for him at different times and on different grounds.

When he mentioned « some advice, » he could only be referring to Clément, who was his neighbor in the Rue de Sèvres before leaving Paris to become head of the Fine Art School in Lyons. Their meeting could have taken place only when Rousseau was just beginning and it is possible that it could explain how Rousseau managed in 1884 to obtain a permit to copy the paintings in the Louvre. And yet Gérôme was the first he mentioned although he could not possibly have been in contact with him. There lies an impassable abyss between Rousseau and the baron Gérôme who, from the pinnacle of his fame, scornfully attacked Manet and the self-taught tollgate attendant who painted for fun. Still, there were good reasons for the claim: Gérôme was, of all artists, the one whom Rousseau had striven to imitate, however unexpected it may seem, whether on a technical level or in the choice of subjects. A detail from Gérôme's celebrated painting *The Cock Fight*, a fragment of the vegetation in the background, isolated and compared with the vegetation painted by Rousseau, amply shows how the latter endeavoured to emulate the academic precision of forms without ever sensing either their conventional coldness or their hardness, which are characteristics of Gérôme, who was both a sculptor and a painter. As for the choice of subject, it is sufficient to recall that Gérôme liked painting wild beasts: *Lioness Meeting a Jaguar, Love in the Wild Beasts' Cage, St. Jérôme Asleep on his Lion* — these are all titles which make us think of Rousseau. But they also point to a link which has largely been overlooked, namely, that the wild animals which are always present in Rousseau's exotic landscapes are connected, through the intermediary of Gérôme's paintings, to none other than Delacroix. Through this deviation, the autodidact set his bearings on the tradition which haunted him but nonetheless remained for him evanescent in spite of all his efforts.

His interest in Bonnat's work once again answered his desire to absorb tradition, the source of his deepest frustration, being this time concerned with portraiture. Was it because Gérôme had painted only the odd portrait that Rousseau looked elsewhere for guidance for his portraits? He found it in Bonnat, in his striking use of black and white. These extreme colors always fascinated Rousseau and he made use of them above all in his portraits, undoubtedly to endow his sitters with greater solemnity, since they are almost without exception dressed in black. The extraordinary gravity which Rousseau was able to infuse

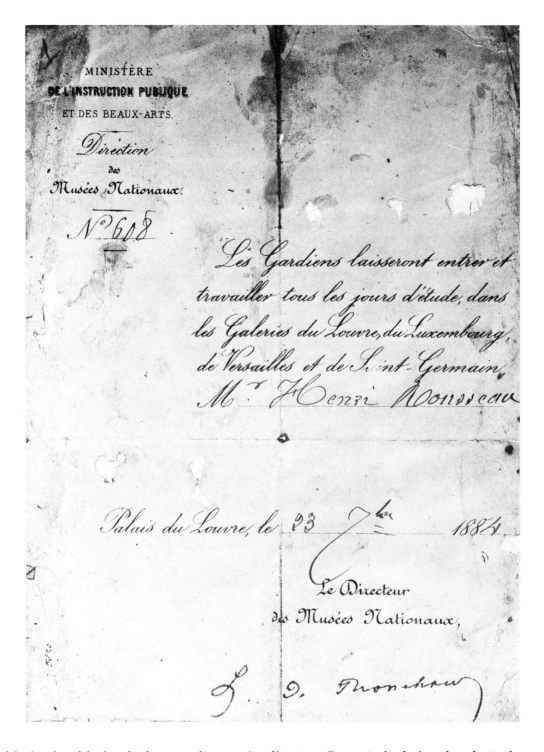

MINISTÈRE
DE L'INSTRUCTION PUBLIQUE
ET DES BEAUX-ARTS.

Direction
des
Musées Nationaux.

N° 608

Les Gardiens laisseront entrer et
travailler tous les jours d'étude, dans
les Galeries du Louvre, du Luxembourg,
de Versailles et de Saint-Germain,
Mr Henri Rousseau

Palais du Louvre, le 23 7bre 1884.

Le Directeur
des Musées Nationaux,

L. D. Monchaw

into black, that black which, according to Apollinaire, Gauguin had already admired, reached its apex in *Boy on the Rocks*, that most unusual commission which is believed to be the portrait of a dead child. Once again, in his contact with academic painting, he firmly believed himself to be abiding by its commandments. Yet he deviated from them and unwittingly transcended them without ever being aware of his achievement.

Boy on the Rocks, 1895–97. Oil on canvas, 21¾″ × 18″ (55.4 × 45.7 cm)
National Gallery of Art, Washington D.C. The Chester Dale Collection

Cockfight, by Léon Gérôme (Detail)
Louvre Museum, Paris

Woman Walking in a Tropical Forest
(Detail) See page 15

Next to the first pressclipping Rousseau wrote in his «notebook of various days»: «Beginning of the year 1885, the two canvases *Italian Dance* and *Sunset* were shown at the Salon: one was slashed with a penknife, then I was cheated out of a compensation, so that I showed it again at the group called the "Refusés" which took place in June.»

Vague indications, floating titles of the events. Which exactly were the salons in question? The salon with no further qualification was that of the Artistes Français. The group of the «Refusés» was the opposition, the advent of modernity, the scandal of *The Picnic*, but all this took place twenty years before. Always the same division and in this division,

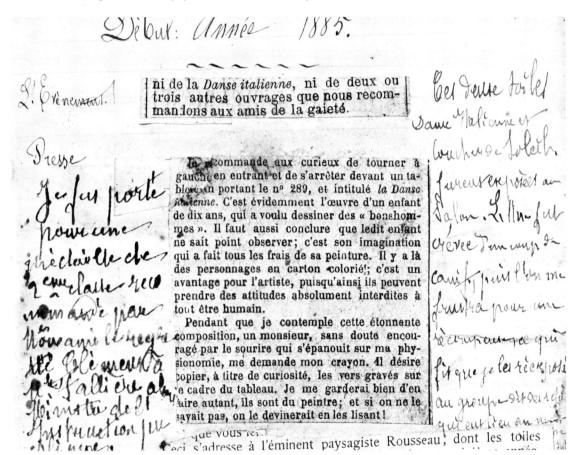

ni de la *Danse italienne*, ni de deux ou trois autres ouvrages que nous recommandons aux amis de la gaieté.

Je recommande aux curieux de tourner à gauche en entrant et de s'arrêter devant un tableau portant le n° 289, et intitulé *la Danse italienne*. C'est évidemment l'œuvre d'un enfant de dix ans, qui a voulu dessiner des « bonshommes ». Il faut aussi conclure que ledit enfant ne sait point observer; c'est son imagination qui a fait tous les frais de sa peinture. Il y a là des personnages en carton colorié; c'est un avantage pour l'artiste, puisqu'ainsi ils peuvent prendre des attitudes absolument interdites à tout être humain.

Pendant que je contemple cette étonnante composition, un monsieur, sans doute encouragé par le sourire qui s'épanouit sur ma physionomie, me demande mon crayon. Il désire copier, à titre de curiosité, les vers gravés sur le cadre du tableau. Je me garderai bien d'en faire autant, ils sont du peintre; et si on ne le savait pas, on le devinerait en les lisant!

...que vous... Ceci s'adresse à l'éminent paysagiste Rousseau, dont les toiles

supreme irony of fate, Rousseau's imprecision straight away placed his art: in the rift that has been opened up, nowhere.

So, already from his first steps, he revealed his own inner split: tempted by an academic subject dear to those coveting the Rome Award, he painted an *Italian Dance*; but simultaneously tempted by Impressionist attitudes, he painted, for his personal delectation, a *Sunset*. This ambivalence runs through his entire output and only lessens toward the end, when the pleasure of painting takes priority over the determination to follow preordained models, in other words, when nature stifled in him all aspirations to culture.

The verb « to create, » in the way Rousseau used it, was not the customary romantic synonym for « to paint. » It had a much deeper meaning and defined a distinct pictorial category. Rousseau made it clear by compiling a list, title after title, of a number of his canvases, setting them apart from his drawings and landscapes, which he grouped only under generic headings. If he insisted on such a distinction, it was because he graded his works strictly according to their subject matter. The first paintings to be named were creations. They alone were entitled to such a label, which was worth its weight in gold: a page of Rousseau's accounts book listing the sales to Vollard in 1910 shows that he was pricing such creations ten times higher than the landscapes.

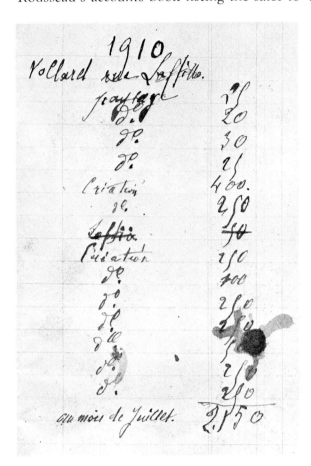

It is true that the creations were also much larger canvases, more polished, but above all much more elaborate in terms of subject matter. And it was precisely their subject that made them so much more valuable. Rousseau rated them as his paramount achievements. In fact, he would select a model and then proceed to embroider on this borrowed canvas, adding his own inventions, conceiving complex scenes which he believed to be imitations of mythological and allegorical scenes, so much so that, from creation to creation, a random iconographic choice, and all of his own making, will run through his entire work, a living reflection of the pomp and ceremony dying out in those same years at the Salon des Artistes Français. There was a side of painting which the Impressionists had rejected: Rousseau welcomed it and invested it with his greatest aspirations. Not too sure of himself when he set out to produce a creation, he took intricate precautions and gathered ample documentation. What is more, he endeavoured to penetrate the spirit of the academic rules in order to submit his own pictorial ways to them. This will to identify with a world which is utterly alien to him presided over all his creations. The starting point of their construction are two clashing languages, one that is his own, direct and ingenuous, and another that stems from academic codifications which regulate even the minutest details. Because of that uncommon encounter, the creations are definitely Rousseau's most surprising works and cannot be fully grasped without some knowledge of their sources. A case in point is the *Happy Quartet*, modelled on Gérôme's *Innocence*. Rousseau did not copy; he extracted selected elements: man, woman, cherub, pet. Yet, in so doing, he altered their meaning: the cherub plays an active part in the scene, and the doe turns into a dog, symbol of fidelity, necessary to this allegory of love with

31

its eternal characters which Rousseau made up out of the plot of *Innocence*. But all his efforts to concentrate on the borrowed elements, such as nudes or cherub, were in vain. Their forms took a grotesque turn because he found it impossible to articulate the academic language correctly, thus baring his clumsiness more blatantly than ever. The iconography for which he cared so much, tributary to a different context, degenerated into parody. But all around it the greenery came into its own: the vast mass of trees, freely worked out, shimmering in chromatic vibrations, embodied the true meaning of the picture conceived to be an image of happiness. Thus Rousseau, much against his will, left Gérôme behind while providing us with the most explicit example of the inner contrast from which his pictures drew their powerful thrust.

Innocence by Léon Gérôme, 1852. Oil on canvas
Musée Massey, Tarbes, France

HAPPY QUARTET (ADAM AND EVE), 1902
Oil on canvas, 37″ × 22½″ (93.5 × 57 cm). Private collection

Of all the drawings which Rousseau ever made, two hundred, he tells us in 1895, only a dozen or so have come down to us. This is hardly anything, all the more so because some are only torn bits of paper, mere scraps, and yet they are preserved as most precious relics. If Picasso and Kandinsky insisted on owning paintings by Rousseau, Morandi preferred his drawings. Picasso was attracted by the shock-impact of Rousseau's canvases. Kandinsky, who had, already in 1912, included him in the Blaue Reiter Almanac, saw in his instinctive realism both the antipode and the equivalent of abstract art. As for Morandi, he cherished in these drawings the slow emergence of the object under observation. And indeed, there was not the least trace of flourish in Rousseau's line, rather the patient insistence of the eye leading the hand. Drawing paved the way to observation, source of pictorial data. The shy and gentle touch of Rousseau's beginnings were but the trace of hachured outlines. Very valid in bold landscapes, it lost its usefulness when required to gain in amplitude to define a form and convey its volume. In other words, Rousseau's drawings can be related only to his landscapes or, to be precise, to the vegetation that fills them. Only there — is it because it had been formed by drawing — does his hand display a faultless assurance. Everywhere else daring thrusts alternate with unexpected repentances, so much so that singular disparities can coexist within the same picture. Perfectly at ease when he painted trees, Rousseau stiffened any time he was faced with a problem of linear perspective and he became positively clumsy any time he

PORTRAIT OF ROUSSEAU'S SECOND WIFE WITH OIL LAMP, 1902–3. Oil on canvas, 9″ × 7″ (23 × 19 cm) Louvre Museum, Paris. Collection Pablo Picasso

FARMYARD, 1896–98. Oil on canvas, 9½″ × 13″ (24 × 33 cm)
Collection: Nina Kandinsky, Neuilly-sur-Seine. This painting appears in the «Blaue Reiter»

THE PAINTER AND HIS MODEL, 1900–5. Oil on canvas, 22″ × 25⅝″ (56.5 × 65 cm)
Collection: Nina Kandinsky, Neuilly-sur-Seine

VIEW OF GENTILLY SEEN FROM THE BIÈVRE, 1895. Oil on canvas, $14^{1}/_{8}'' \times 18^{1}/_{8}''$ (36×46 cm)
Tate Gallery, London

touched on the human face and had to portray a person. He panicked in circumstances from which trivial academic routines were bound to emerge triumphant, and if he ended by winning in his own way, he did so at the cost of considerable effort. A glance at his portraits reveals that on all hands and faces the paint layer has grown thicker and heavier by dint of endless repainting. The case of his landscapes is quite different. There Rousseau's gesture does not labor under any constraint. He painted slowly, assiduously, as he did every time he made up his mind to exhibit a landscape, and he did so regularly at the Salon des Indépendants. Alternatively, he worked fast, the technique betraying then the speed of the execution. This happened with the numerous landscapes intended for sale. There he began by covering the

SNOWSCAPE, c. 1892. Oil on canvas, 13″ × 18⅛″ (33 × 46 cm)
Private collection

canvas with wide brushstrokes, returning over this first-color layer with hurriedly applied minute touches. He sometimes even jotted down extraordinary oil sketches on the spot. The more experience he gained, the longer he liked to linger on the landscapes worked out from his sketches. In this way, landscapes led Rousseau to an ever-increasing plastic freedom. Except in his early days, he only once or twice copied a model, some print or trivial illustration, to rework it into a landscape. Usually, he started from nature, which he had observed no less closely than the Impressionists but for the sheer pleasure of doing so, without ever asking himself why and how he was doing it. No artist was more sensitive than he to the flutter of leaves or to their stillness, to their differences and their intertwining

HOUSE IN PARIS SUBURB, 1902
Oil on canvas, 13⅜″ × 18⅛″ (34 × 46 cm)
Museum of Art, Carnegie Institute
Pittsburgh, Pennsylvania
This painting belonged in the
past to the American painter Max Weber

These two pencil drawings,
which are in fact pieces of torn drawings
(one is 4″ × 2¼″ - 10.2 × 5.8 cm
the other 3⅞″ × 1¼″ - 9.8 × 4.4 cm)
belonged to the Italian painter
Giorgio Morandi

38

LANDSCAPE WITH MANOR, 1890–95. Oil on canvas, 13″ × 16″ (33 × 41 cm)
Collection Christophe Tzara, Sceaux, France

form. The virgin forests which he painted toward the end of his life were only the projection on an imaginary scale of those same observations in his daily life, experiences enhanced by fascination. All this indicates that landscapes are the core of Rousseau's work. Yet, valuing only his creations, he never seemed to grow fully aware of the landscapes' importance and was always ready to barter them against modest commodities. A fair amount of them were found after his death in the households of local traders, astounded at the prices they fetched or disappointed: «When you think that the old nut left us all that junk to pay his debts! Sure it went straight to the flea market together with the other rags.»

Such was the fate of a great many of Rousseau's landscapes but also, and this is much more surprising, of some creations. *The Sleeping Gypsy* was discovered in 1923 in the workshop of a plumber in Paris and *War* was found in 1944, all rolled up, in the barn of a farmer: marginal events that show up the vastness of the no-man's-land in which Rousseau had toiled.

REPRESENTATIVES OF FOREIGN POWERS COME TO SALUTE THE REPUBLIC AS A PEACEFUL GESTURE, 1907
Oil on canvas, 51″ × 63″ (130 × 162 cm). Louvre Museum, Paris. Collection Pablo Picasso

«When I painted the Union of the People *where the representatives of foreign powers come to salute the Republic as a peaceful gesture, I was quite unable to get out of the exhibition for the crowd of people around me who wanted to shake my hand and congratulate me. And do you know why? Because it was at the time of the Hague Conference, and I hadn't even thought of it. But that's how it happened. The letters I received from all over the world, Belgium, Germany, Russia, well everywhere really!»*

The pictures quoted by Rousseau were all, without a single exception, exhibited at the Salon des Indépendants, and in the catalogue their titles always headed the list of his sendings. Not only do they show his commitment, they were also sizewise the most imposing and consequently the most commented on by the press. In the descriptions given in such reviews, more often than not disparaging, we can glean traces of works that have vanished. Only one of these titles appears at first sight to be an exception: *Tiger Pursuing Explorers.* In fact, it was Rousseau who was mistaken in his quotation, and this slip is most revealing.

The picture in question was exhibited in 1891 under the title *Surprised!* If the leaping beast clearly manifests surprise, this title, made of a past participle followed by an exclamation point, proved so disconcerting that it was never linked to the actual painting, which was known until recently as *The Storm in the Jungle.* This second title was obviously a chance invention at the sight of the picture, and yet, in mentioning a jungle, it did establish the right relation between this early work and the virgin forests that made Rousseau famous toward the end of his life. It is indeed in this picture that the exotic vegetation is first seen, and right from the start, it is displayed on a canvas whose dimensions are quite exceptional for Rousseau, as it measures 4 by 5 ft. How did this self-taught painter manage to come to terms with such a large surface? The answer is both simple and significant: Rousseau made use of a pantograph. Assisted by this mechanical enlarger, he was able to draw the outlines of all the forms from an illustration, found perhaps in one of those children's books which he is known to have used later for the same purpose. Once the outlines had been traced, all he had to do was to color the whole, and he did so to his heart's delight. Swamped by this chromatic exuberance, the small insignificant image providing the scaffolding of this picture has altogether vanished. The clumsy draftsman had been brushed aside by the pantograph to give full freedom of action to the born colorist who worked a miracle, so much so that he startled another artist, Félix Valloton, who happened to report for «Le Journal Suisse»: «With each year that passes, Mr. Rousseau grows more and more stunning . . . he crushes everything. His tiger catching his prey unaware must be seen; it is the alpha and the omega of painting, and so disconcerting that the most deeply rooted convictions waver and falter in front of such self-sufficiency and such childlike candor. Not everybody laughs, by the way, and some who may have felt like laughing are soon silenced. It is always marvelous to see a belief, whatever it may be, so mercilessly expressed. As for myself, I hold his efforts in sincere esteem and I prefer them a hundredfold to the deplorable errors displayed in the other paintings hung nearby . . .»

Now Rousseau knew only too well what he had done to make his picture. He knew that he had cheated. And if the bizarre phrasing of the title showed that he intended to conceal his misdeed, the slip repressed this misleading utterance and brought to the forefront the true title, that of the illustration blown up by the pantograph in which the tiger was undoubtedly chasing some explorers whom the enlargement had excluded from the painting.

*　*　*

Henri Rousseau

SURPRISED! 1891
Oil on canvas
51″ × 63″ (130 × 162 cm)
National Gallery, London

43

BABY'S PARTY, 1903. Oil on canvas, 39⅜″ × 31⅞″ (100 × 81 cm). Kunstverein, Winterthur

Rousseau once again resorted to the pantograph to disguise his shortcomings in *The Centenary of Independence*, where the dancers who form the circle have been outlined according to a mechanically enlarged model. At the very beginning of his career, painting on a wood panel, he had occasionally traced the outlines with a metallic point. But at the time his technique was heavy, his colors murky and the picture sizes small. Now, and the mechanical enlarger played a not inconspicuous part, he ventured into large sizes and abandoned the tiny splintered touches in favor of flat brushstrokes, while keeping an eye on his colors, which had become bright and luminous. He himself said:

> Puvis de Chavannes told me: «Monsieur Rousseau, I don't in general like the brash coloring that one sees here at the Indépendants, but I very much like yours because it is right.» He had in mind my *Centenary of Independence*. There were *sixty-two different tones in the paper lanterns.*

Never did Rousseau hesitate in applying a color; on the other hand, he never knew how to place a volume in space. Knowing nothing of linear perspective, he got out of trouble by expedients which, in the long run, became compulsive mannerisms. One of them is blatantly obvious in *The Centenary of Independence.* Knowing full well that he was incapable of drawing a foot resting on the ground, a position which articulated several spatial planes, he worked things out in such a way that the feet of the characters invented by him were sunk in the grass. This happened with the group set in the foreground on the right, and this sly contrivance is offset by the feet of the dancers, perfectly articulated in space by virtue of the pantograph. Rousseau's painting was indeed singular: in it, disparate, even contradictory, structures were brought together without in the least upsetting the whole. On the contrary, their disparities and their contradictions, sustained by just the right colors, surreptitiously activate the sight and resolve themselves into plastic forces. Hence the duality of Rousseau's vision, which is simultaneously synthetic and analytic: a minute leaf can be given the perfectly legible structure of a form seen at close quarters, while a nearby human figure, in spite of its stature, can be painted as a distant form whose details are blurred. For Rousseau, distance does not determine the aspect of forms. Neither space nor likeness are their common denominator: a most carefully described form can be placed near another, utterly unreal, devoid of any logical foundation and needed only on plastic grounds; yet, set side by side, they enhance the validity of the whole. Such is the case of *The Centenary of Independence*: the immaculate white bush on the left stresses the overall fairy-tale atmosphere. Finally, Rousseau deals in the same way with the problems of perspective: he treats the various portions of the picture in the same cavalier fashion, multiplying the viewpoints as a matter of course. Without being in the least aware of it, he then skirted the quests of Cubism, which he solved with a beautifully inconsequential candor. Instinctively, he placed the trunk of the central tree in the axis of the vanishing point at which converged poles and flags; yet at the same time, by a mere interplay of colors and optical fitting of forms, he suggested a second direction, which, almost like a diagonal beam, led the eye across the picture, from the group in the foreground on the right, through the ronde, up to the children in the farthest background on the left. It may well be an improvised effect, the most heretical of all heretical solutions, but what an enrichment of the pictorial space!

And what an unexpected impact on the beholders: «I can honestly say that I had quite a success. Look! The year I painted my allegory of *The Centenary of Independence* I had shown our ancestors in breeches dancing to celebrate the dawn of freedom and I had inscribed in a corner of my composition, on the frame, the first verses of the old French song: "Beside my blond lass, what a joy, a joy, a joy . . ." Well, my dear friend, when I turned up for the opening, everybody was dancing in front of my picture singing: "Beside my blond lass . . ." Everybody was happy.»

«My allegory,» said Rousseau. It follows that the meaning of the picture had been deliberately set on a conceptual level. Through the concrete image Rousseau aimed at an abstract level. From the particular he ascended to the universal. This was an operation which inevitably involved his culture. But what was, in fact, his culture? There can be only one answer to this question: for him, the World's Fair of 1889 is the only substitute for culture. All that he had seen within its precincts had marked him for life. The manifold reality of faraway lands, history, sciences, art, the great events of the day, this huge mass of information had been all of a sudden unfolded in front of him, although circumscribed and, above all, adjusted to his mentality, which was very much that of the average Frenchman. Lacking the power of discrimination which was a by-product of culture, Rousseau was constantly spurred by his vivid sensitivity and by the all-embracing curiosity that often tantalizes self-made men. Because posterity has proclaimed him a great artist, we tend to approach him in the wrong way: we look for him at the Louvre while he is to be found at the Champs de Mars, at that solemn funfair at the foot of the newly erected Eiffel Tower, where five continents have got together, each with its races and its vegetation, its sights and its deeds. For six crowded months, the World's Fair was the only topic worth talking about for the whole of Paris. As for Rousseau, it was the out-and-out pivotal experience of his life. His exaltation was such that he even went as far as writing a flippant comedy, most tellingly called «A Visit to the Exhibition of 1889.» He was no longer the fellow who, through the practice of painting, sensed the existence of another world quite unlike his own, set apart, sealed for all those who, like him, had never been taught how to enter it. Now he had learned it all and all by himself, all that a painter had to know. His comedy paraded his newly acquired culture.

Not unnaturally, the allegory of *The Centenary of Independence* leaned heavily on the 1889 Exhibition. As its date coincided with the centenary of the French Revolution, there had been a profusion of mass festivities, popular and patriotic, recalling the spirit of 1789. Hence, in Rousseau's allegory, the opposition: Phrygian bonnets/powdered periwigs, joyful upsurge of the people/motionless aristocrats frozen in the lower-right-hand corner. This confrontation was made explicit by the picture as a whole, most ostensibly revealing its sources: in its very center, there flutter, fraternally crossed, the national flag and the colors of the City of Paris, plain blue and red without heraldic overlays, brought back and made fashionable once again precisely by the World's Fair of 1889.

*

*   *

THE CENTENARY OF INDEPENDENCE, 1892. Oil on canvas, 44″ × 61⅞″ (112 × 156.5 cm)
Private collection

The picture was exhibited at the 1892 Salon des Indépendants with the following caption:

> *The people dance around the two Republics, that of 1872 and that of 1892, holding hands to the tune of the old French song «Auprès de ma blonde qu'il fait bon, fait bon dormir.» («Beside my blond lass, what a joy, a joy to sleep.»)*

The World's Fair closed its gates in October 1889 and in March 1890 Rousseau already exhibited at the Salon des Indépendants his self-portrait which he called *Myself. Portrait-Landscape.* On the festive background of a ship dressed in rainbow fashion, standing upright against the sky, the excise man proclaims that he is an artist: Rembrandtlike hat, palette in one hand, brush in the other. All dressed in black, his white cuff hardly protruding from the sleeve of his jacket, he appears to have imbued this impeccable attire with that dignity which his contemporaries had seen in him. He is here the respectable artist. Graying beard, intense gaze. Reality and wishful thinking merge. The portrait thus reached a deep truth that no one could have guessed in 1890: this man was a great artist.

At the Salon des Indépendants, Rousseau's self-portrait became a laughingstock: « The artist, moved no doubt by an excess of modesty, has painted himself no taller than a dwarf, with an outsize head, bursting perhaps with profound thoughts . . . The best thing to do is to feel at the same time moved and disarmed.» Another reaction: « I found it extremely difficult to come to terms with Monsieur Henri Rousseau whom I shall call, if I may, the sensation at the Indépendants. M. Rousseau is bent on renewing the art of painting. The *Portrait-Landscape* is his own invention and I would advise him to take out a patent on it, as unscrupulous characters are quite capable of using it.»

But Rousseau was insensitive to the irony, so much so that in 1907 he wrote in all sincerity: « I am the Inventor of the portrait-landscape as the press has pointed out . . . » He had, no doubt, according to his faith in his art, always read all the mockeries collected in his scrapbook in this way. Impervious to irony, he was most sensitive to praise: « The Sincerity of all my works is widely recognized.» The capital S underpinned this statement. And who could object? Stubbornly Rousseau awaited his day of glory. He compelled his painting to declare it in all its facets. Image-deep symbols, easy to decode.

There is first of all the juxtaposition and exchange between himself and the Eiffel Tower, which was exceedingly famous in those days. Himself and the Eiffel Tower, linked by the festoon of flags and supreme splendor of celebrity, joint festivity and chromatic focus of the picture, counterpoint of the nearby black, source of light pressed against the artist's body, as if it were its shadow, but an inverted one, shadow transmuted in radiance and linking with the Eiffel Tower, itself set within the artist's shadow. The floating balloon and the flowing Seine: two infinities, space and time, evoked to serve as a framework for the entire picture. The apotheosis of Rousseau.

His self-portrait, his double truer than himself. It was a painting with which Rousseau lived long after completing it. Two names were inscribed on the palette: Clémence and Joséphine. Clémence, his first wife who had died in 1888, and Joséphine, whom he married only in 1899, long after painting his self-portrait. Rousseau then obliterated a shorter name, most certainly his own, and replaced it with that of Joséphine. This picture, dating from his widowhood, witnessed new events. But Rousseau, sentimental as he was, did not rub out the name of Clémence. Then, in 1901 when he was appointed teacher at the Ecole Philotechnique, he added to his buttonhole the ribbon indicating the Order of academic distinction. Rousseau requested of his portrait that it progress through life as he did, and never stopped updating it.

MYSELF. PORTRAIT-LANDSCAPE, 1890. Oil on canvas, 56″ × 43½″ (143 × 110 cm)
Narodni Galerie, Prague

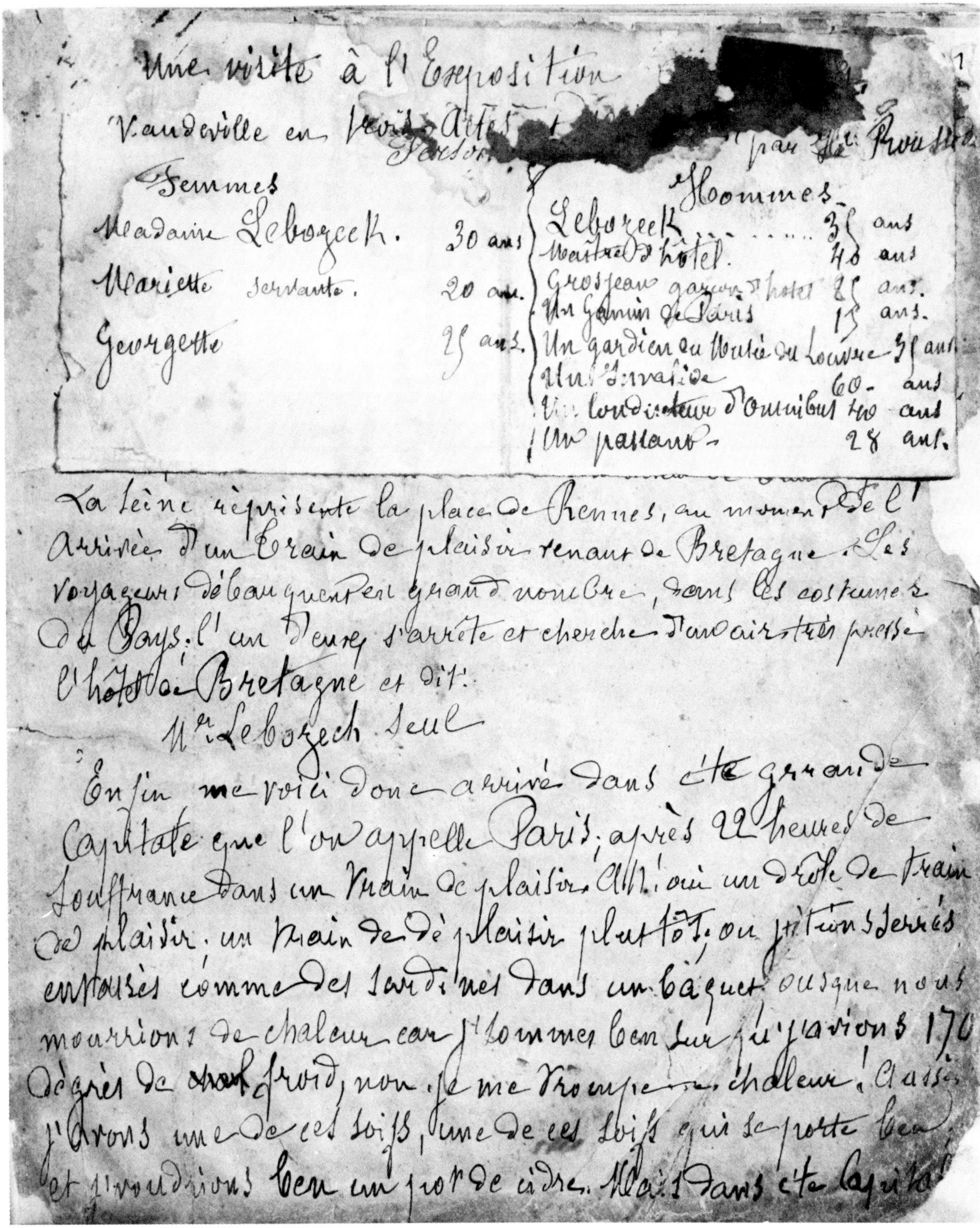

Une visite à l'Exposition

Vaudeville en trois Actes   par M. Rousseau

Femmes		Hommes	
Madame Lebozech.	30 ans	Lebozech	35 ans
		Maître d'hôtel.	40 ans
Mariette servante.	20 ans	Grosjean garçon d'hôtel	25 ans.
		Un Gamin de Paris	15 ans.
Georgette	25 ans.	Un gardien au Musée du Louvre	35 ans.
		Une Servante	60 ans
		Un conducteur d'Omnibus	40 ans
		Un passant	28 ans.

La scène représente la place de Rennes, au moment de l'arrivée d'un train de plaisir venant de Bretagne. Les voyageurs débarquent en grand nombre, dans les costumes du Pays. l'un d'eux s'arrête et cherche d'un air très pressé l'hôtel de Bretagne et dit :

Mr Lebozech. seul

Enfin me voici donc arrivé dans cette grande Capitale que l'on appelle Paris; après 22 heures de souffrance dans un train de plaisir. Ah! oui un drôle de train de plaisir, un train de déplaisir plutôt, où j'étions serrés entassés comme des sardines dans un baquet ousque nous mourrions de chaleur car j'tommes ben sûr qu'j'avions 170 degrés de chaud froid, non je me trompe, de chaleur! aussi j'avons une de ces soifs, une de ces soifs qui se porte ben et j'voudrions ben un pot de cidre. Mais dans cette Capitale

First page of Rousseau's vaudeville manuscript « A Visit to the Paris World's Fair of 1889 »

Last of the 51ˢᵗ is a picture, now lost, which was shown at the Salon des Indépendants in 1893 with the following caption: « After long battles, the regiment was entirely decimated; the poor invalid is the only one left alive to save the standard under which our elders have conquered so much glory. »

This caption is most telling: Rousseau's intentions were once again turned to the academic repertory, rich in military scenes all through the nineteenth century. (Meissonnier springs naturally to mind.) But the title itself yields a subsidiary piece of information: the 51ˢᵗ Infantry Regiment was the one in which the conscript Rousseau had served and which he had joined again at Dreux during the war of 1870, without, however, reaching the front line. These are the facts. But, already during Rousseau's lifetime, they had been so distorted that his extremely inconspicuous biography had disappeared in a legendary blaze. In 1913 Apollinaire wrote: « Wars have played an important part in the life of the Douanier. In 1870 the coolheadedness of Sergeant Rousseau saved the town of Dreux from the horrors of civil war. He loved to recall the details of this admirable deed, and his broken old voice had a singularly proud ring when he was telling how a multitude of civilians and soldiers had acclaimed him shouting: "Long live Sergeant Rousseau." »

Who was letting his fancy roam, Apollinaire or Rousseau? We shall never know. At all events, the painting exhibited by the Douanier in 1893 related a similar story, with the sole difference that through the image of the only survivor, the honor of Rousseau's entire regiment was saved in a terrible defeat. This defeat was considered, probably because of Rousseau's own muted hint, part of the ill-fated French expedition to Mexico in support of Emperor Maximilian. If his own regiment, glorified in the picture, had not actually taken part in that expedition, it is quite possible that, being in the army at the time when the survivors from Mexico were brought back to France, he may have met some of them or heard their stories retold in barracks rooms. The link between Mexico and himself was therefore somewhat less than tenuous. And yet it proved quite sufficient to create a pretty solid legend: Rousseau had quite definitely fought in the Mexican war, thus gaining firsthand knowledge of the tropics. The evidence was to be found in his exotic landscapes. Curiously enough, art was called upon to occult the true life story and to give credibility to the legend. All this happened because the false biography somehow managed to anchor Rousseau's paintings which otherwise floated utterly unattached. It made their explanation possible, by erasing their strangeness and replacing that by the normal relation which art was supposed to have with nature. Legends located Rousseau in this familiar vision of art, while the truth expelled him from it. Reporting in « Comoedia » of 1910 on his visit to Rousseau's studio, Arsène Alexandre stated categorically: « It did not take much to make him confess that he had never set foot beyond the hothouses of the Jardin des Plantes. » Apollinaire did not believe a word of it, and in the tribute which he paid to Rousseau in « Les Soirées de Paris, » three years after his death in 1913, he reverted to the legend of the Mexican journey: « Questioned about those days, all he seemed to remember were some fruits which he had seen and which the soldiers were forbidden to eat. But his eyes had kept other memories: tropical jungles, monkeys . . . » The books on Rousseau published over the years have repeated the same version, right up to the sixties when at long last Rousseau's biography was restored to its rightful place, previously usurped by legends.

THE ARTILLERYMEN, 1893. Oil on canvas, 28¼″ × 35⅜″ (72 × 90 cm)
The Solomon R. Guggenheim Museum, New York

A. J. stands for Alfred Jarry. The author of « Ubu Roi » was instrumental in launching the painting tollgate attendant. The fateful meeting must have taken place some time in 1893. Rousseau was almost fifty years old; Jarry was twenty. Rousseau was a modest excise man who had recently retired to devote himself at long last to full-time painting. Jarry was a brilliant young man who had come up to Paris to study for his admission to the Ecole Normale and who already frequented the circle around « Le Mercure de France. » There was no bond between them, and they had nothing in common except a single coincidence: they were both born in Laval. And as the actual circumstances of their encounter are still unknown, legends have proliferated to fill the gaps. The fact is that in March 1895 « le Mercure » published an article on Rousseau, the only one of a certain length to praise him unreservedly during his lifetime. A month later Rousseau exhibited Jarry's portrait at the Salon des Indépendants.

Unfortunately, this portrait has vanished, having been destroyed by Jarry himself who riddled it with pistol bullets « for the sheer literary delight of slicing his own image, rolling it up and keeping it in a drawer for the benefit of select visitors, » wrote André Salmon, and Apollinaire added that in 1906, when he saw this portrait, it was partly burned and all that was left was « the very expressive head. »

A portrait which is part-target and part-holocaust, self-immolation in effigy of Ubu. But it had, Rousseau specified, started life as a portrait-genre and, therefore, as an extremely ambitious enterprise aiming at the deep identity of the sitter far beyond his likeness. Rumor has it that, according to Jarry, the Douanier had taken his precautions to ensure this likeness (as he was to do later in painting Apollinaire) by measuring with his brush Jarry's nose, mouth, ears and transferring these measurements straight onto the canvas without bothering at all about their foreshortening. He is also said to have examined the color tubes right up against Jarry's face « to find the exact tone of the flesh. » As for the deep identity, he had chosen to signify it through emblematic figures, such as, in Jarry's case, the famous chameleon, his inseparable companion.

It appears that these attributes, coupled with the unsteady draftsmanship, had a most unexpected impact, « as the tongue of the chameleon was mistaken by a critic for a pen » notes « L'Idée Moderne. » But, according to « Le Gaulois, » such a confusion was quite understandable: « Rousseau has certainly not used his hands to paint this picture . . . If one has not seen his portrait of a man with owls perched on a windowsill in broad daylight; if one has not seen this man made out of zinc, with a dirty face to boot, set against the yellow background drapery on which have been scribbled all sorts of figures and beasts . . . one has not seen anything. » More sedate, the critic of « Le Temps » saw Jarry « seated near a balcony, his eyes black, round and staring, his hair implacably black, in his Sunday best outfit which is also black, stressing once again the earnestness of his usual thoughts. » Finally, as solemn captions were fashionable, even for the pictures shown at a nonconformist exhibition like the Salon des Indépendants, one could read, under Jarry's portrait, the following stanza, exquisitely handwritten on a label stuck in the middle of the gilded frame:

Muses, whose dreaming forehead is a triangle of stone,
Embellish his eyes with your image — so that he will ever please
Those readers striving in their sincere minds
To taste in great delight all the gifts of light.

«But who is the author of this stanza? the painter or the poet?» asked the attentive critic of «Le Temps,» while his colleague of «Le National» cried out: «Go to see the Rousseaus, oh my readers: you'll get your money's worth in fun and laughter.»

A last detail about the Ubulike adventures of this picture: in the catalogue of the Salon des Indépendants, it was entered under the caption *Portrait of Madame A. J.* The printing error, put right by the press reviews, was due to Jarry's exceedingly long hair.

What could this portrait have been like? If we knew it, our judgment, positively different, perhaps even favorable (and why not?) would have modified, corrected, and in any case attenuated the impression made by the reviews of the time. Acting on their own, they preserve intact their persuasive power, while we are doomed to remain speechless, realizing fully this time how strong must have been the shock caused by Rousseau's painting.

War (Detail)

Like a breach opened all of a sudden and straightaway closed again, *War* is the only one of Rousseau's creations (in his personal meaning of the word) whose emergence is fully illuminated by reliable documentation. From the source to the project, and from the project to the definitely completed work, each phase is well known (including all motivations, we may add without fear of error). Rousseau was at that time quite friendly with Jarry and it was to his presence that he owed his sudden assurance, that would vanish as soon as Jarry vanished, to return much later when he met Apollinaire. Twice in his lifetime Rousseau found himself in strangely similar circumstances: the first time he skirted the Symbolist circles in 1894–95, and then, ten years later, because of Apollinaire, he was definitely involved in the Paris avant-garde. And each time, breaking away from his isolation, Rousseau gained new impetus. Surely, there was an ambiguity lingering in his relations with these circles, but the facts are there: at such starry moments, his work touched its summit.

War appeared initially as a lithograph destined for the luxurious magazine «L'Ymagier» which Rémy de Gourmont had just founded, assisted by Jarry. It was published in January 1895, but it is obvious that it had been completed before the painting, which was exhibited in the spring of 1894. There can be no doubt whatsoever that this lithograph had been commissioned from Rousseau to be included in a series of prints of horsemen promoted by the magazine. One of them was a cavalry battle scene by Giorgione which Rousseau must have seen before starting work on his commission. Are we to infer from this assignment that, in the minds of Rémy de Gourmont and Jarry, Rousseau's work belonged to the popular imagery with which «L'Ymagier» appeared to associate it? In any case, he did not at all relish such an association. It was Jarry the intellectual, who loved the popular naïve cartoons; it was Rémy de Gourmont, the belated romantic and scholar who defended their merits. Rousseau admired only academic art. He began by studying Giorgione, from whom he borrowed the idea of the brandished sword; he had been struck by the heap of corpses in the foreground (foregrounds have always been something of a stumbling block in the buildup of his work), but he ended by opting for a very ordinary illustration published in «L'Egalité.» Of his own accord, he added the two trees on the sides and transfigured the horsewoman into a monstrous being, symbol of war. By hook or by crook, with a groping hand, he completed his lithograph (his first and last print). But when he turned to the painting and chose a 6′ 8″ wide canvas, he let his imagination run free. Without bothering about the pantograph or any other kind of crutch, he reached the furthest point of his possibilities.

As soon as Rousseau began to paint, as soon as colors sprang to action, the picture found its inherent order and gained in vigor. He took over the elements of the lithograph with that difference that, in rearranging them, he also decanted them. To set them in their proper new places, he altered the composition. In the lithograph, all forms were converging onto the horse; in the painting there appeared a structure which was very much of his own making and which he had already exploited in *The Centenary of Independence.* With the two large trees on the sides, he created an optical diagonal underlined by the white sword, while at the same time he recentered the composition with the frontality of the horse. This double spatial inflection indirectly served the subject: unhinged, our sight loses the bearings of reality and at once succumbs to the spell of an unwonted universe. Rousseau

A lithograph by Rousseau «War» printed in «L'Ymagier», 1895.   8¾″ × 13″ (22.3 × 33 cm)
National Gallery of Art, Washington D.C. The Rosenwald Collection

the observer here plunged right to the heart of a fantastic vision, which he rotated around a double axis, as he had done with space. The idea of devastation was grafted onto that of battle: the torch set off the sword; the trees exploded in countless splinters. To the feeling of horror awakened by the heap of rotting flesh was added a sense of hairraising exasperation spurred by the repeated presence of frayed forms: the unnaturally long mane that transmuted the horse into a monster, the unkempt hair of the horsewoman, real animal hide, but also her ragged white tunic enhancing the impact of the nearby black. From this sharp contrast gushes forth a wave of terror and, merging with repulsion, drowns the picture in a flood of nightmares.

WAR (Detail)

War, 1894. Oil on canvas, 44⅜″ × 76″ (114 × 195 cm). Louvre Museum, Paris

«At the exhibition of the Independent Artists in 1894, *War* by Monsieur Rousseau was positively the most remarkable painting. Neither a rounded-off achievement nor a perfect picture, this canvas conveys, whatever some may think, a brave endeavor in search of symbols. The artist who has chosen to paint in this way once again manifests his individuality: this work may have seemed strange only because it does not recall anything seen up to now. Is this not a supreme quality? Why should strangeness give birth to mockery? Even when the attempt has not borne the expected fruits, and this is not the case here, any scoffing would be completely unjustified, it would only betray a petty mind. By and large in our society, there prevails a habit of classifying, numbering, labeling and enclosing all things in separate cases. By hook or by crook, each parcel of creation must be forced into such a case. If not, the beholder, disconcerted and vexed by his inability to understand, hastens to decree the absurdity of anything that has remained impervious to his mind. In other words, and apparently in all modesty, he dares declare: "I don't understand it, therefore it is inane." For all the progress of the human species, a progress made tangible by the telegraph and the telephone, the bicycle and scenic railways, it is quite certain that we are much less open-minded than our forefathers in the Middle Ages, for they showed their deep regard for misunderstood personalities in saying: "Credo quia absurdum."

«Monsieur Rousseau has shared the fate of all innovators. He stems from himself; he has the merit, nowadays quite rare, of being absolutely personal. He strives toward a new art. This endeavor, very interesting on the whole in spite of some shortcomings, shows great qualities in some of its aspects, such as the black spots which are exceptionally beautiful. The composition unfolded horizontally has been well understood. The immense black horse speeding at full gallop and stretching across the whole width of the canvas, is far from being banal. It is even a high-style spot. This horse is ridden by war, brandishing in her right hand a sword and in her left a flaming torch. The ground is littered with the corpses of ordinary humans, fat and thin, destitute, proletarians. They are all dead or dying. In those who are still breathing, horror is at its height. Nature has been altogether destroyed. Or rather there remain a couple of trees bereft of all their leaves, one gray, the other black; and ravens, attracted by the stench of blood, have descended in force to savor the flesh of the war victims. The ground is buried under misshapen wreckage, the earth has no greenery left, not even the tiniest blade of grass. This picture conveys admirably the desolation caused by the irreparable disaster; in a brief while there will be nothing left alive. Fires, as the distant glow on the horizon betokens, will achieve the cruel deed begun by arms. In a moment all will be forever dead. . . . And war rides impassive as ever, inexorable, implacable like a divinity. War will be replenished with bloodshed. Nothing can stop her frenzied progress. What an obsession, what a nightmare! What a harrowing impression of insurmountable sorrow! It would take a person of quite bad faith to dare proclaim that the man who is able to suggest such ideas is not an artist.»

L. Roy: «Mercure de France,» March 1895

Rousseau put down on paper his deepest conviction: «He has improved himself more and more in the original style adopted by him and he is in the process of becoming one of our best realist painters.» The two principal propositions of this phrase are linked by a causal relation which is worth examining at close quarters. What is the meaning of «original style»? What is the meaning of «realist painter»? And how do they come together in Rousseau's mind? One of the most famous paintings of all times will help us find the answer: *The Sleeping Gypsy.* Discovered in 1923, when Rousseau's work was much less known than it is today, it was decried by some as a forgery, a farce whose author was said to be Derain. As the rumors concerning this discovery spread at the height of Surrealism, this picture was promptly proclaimed an evidence of the «chance meeting between two distant realities on an ill-suited plane.» On the other hand, those who were of the opinion that it was painted by Rousseau considered it a decisive step beyond realism and an opening onto the surreal, and this view has long prevailed. And when the authenticity of the picture was confirmed by the discovery of a letter in which Rousseau was offering it for sale, this interpretation gained in authority as there seemed to be no esthetic category into which it could fit. And yet, even a scant awareness of Rousseau's vision makes quite a different interpretation absolutely imperative. For Rousseau *The Sleeping Gypsy* was a realistic picture. The logical order with which the scene was set was stated in the letter which he had sent in 1898 to the Mayor of Laval: he had deliberately painted a wandering black girl who, exhausted by fatigue, had fallen asleep. Her mandolin, a common accessory, was by her side and so was her jar, which fulfilled a very precise function. The parenthesis which Rousseau opened to explain that the jar «contains drinking water» made this clear and added yet another detail in the name of realism: as the action takes place in a «completely arid» desert and the water within the container cannot be seen, it was necessary to insist on its existence. Was it not the only means of survival? Logically, the jar is therefore a central element. That is why Rousseau underlined the word. Up to there, everything was unimpeachably coherent. Then, all of a sudden, the carefully constructed logical order goes haywire: a lion happens to be passing by, sniffs the sleeping girl, and does not gobble her up. All credibility vanishes into thin air only to reappear in the next sentence, which says that all is «bathed in moonlight.» What is the meaning of this sudden collapse of realism which Rousseau did not even notice? The reason for it all was that it was precisely at this point that Rousseau brought into his picture the elements gleaned from the iconography of academic art: he borrowed them wholesale, while at the same time stripping them of their logical order. Reset in the new context which he had worked out on his own, they immediately shed their coherence and their realism, but Rousseau was hardly aware of this, because for him the Academy was law. If Gérôme found it right and proper to paint a *Saint Jérôme Asleep on his Lion*, why should the wandering black girl not fall asleep beside another lion, all the more so because the latter was on his home ground in the desert into which the girl had strayed? All this goes to show that, for Rousseau, this painting was entirely realistic. But at the same time, it belonged to an original style because it had nothing to do with the flat mimicry of a landscape but bore the marks of a superior realism, which, in Rousseau's mind, was the equivalent of intricate academic iconography. And therefore this original style, typical of those pictures which he called creations, warrants his success as a realist painter.

THE SLEEPING GYPSY, 1897. Oil on canvas, 51″ × 79″ (129.5 × 200.5 cm)
Museum of Modern Art, New York. Gift of Mrs. Simon Guggenheim

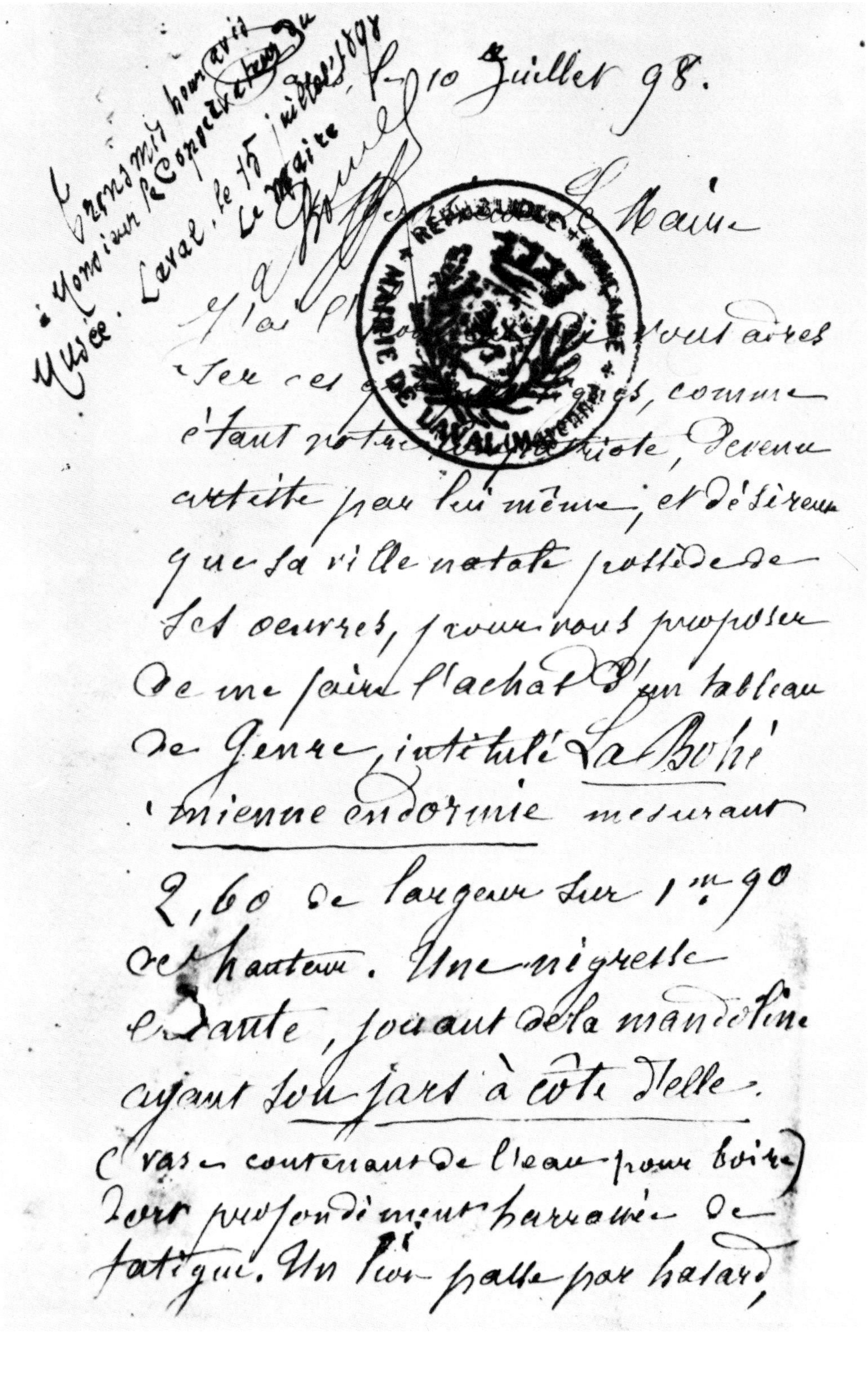

Transmis pour avis à Monsieur le Conservateur du Musée. Laval, le 15 juillet 1898 Le Maire

10 Juillet 98.

Monsieur le Maire

J'ai l'honneur de vous adresser ces quelques lignes, comme étant votre compatriote, devenu artiste par lui même, et désireux que sa ville natale possède de ses oeuvres, pour vous proposer de me faire l'achat d'un tableau de genre intitulé La Bohémienne endormie mesurant 2,60 de largeur sur 1m90 de hauteur. Une négresse errante, jouant de la mandoline ayant son jars à côté d'elle. (vase contenant de l'eau pour boire) dort profondément harrassée de fatigue. Un lion passe par hasard,

Rousseau's letter to the Mayor of Laval

la fleur, et ne la dévore pas. Bien un effet de lune, très poétique: La Seine se passe dans un désert complètement aride. La Bohémienne est vêtue à l'orientale. —

Je te laisserai de 2000 à 1800 francs, parce que je serai heureux que la ville de Laval ait un souvenir de l'un de ses enfants.

Dans l'Espoir, que mon offre sera accepté avec faveur, agréez, Monsieur Le Maire, l'Assurance de ma considération distinguée.

Henri Rousseau
artiste peintre
3 rue Vercingetorix.
Paris.

«As a distinctive feature, he sports a bushy beard and has long been a member of the Indépendants.» These words are so preposterous that they make one smile. But this is only a misleading appearance. In fact, this sentence is simply tautological. The bushy beard and the Salon des Indépendants are only different ways of uttering the same statement: «I am an artist.» And that is the outstanding distinctive feature of Rousseau. The Rembrandt hat which he wore in his *Portrait-Landscape* and put on again when he was to be photographed, makes the same point. As an artist, he rightly identifies with the Salon des Indépendants, as this was his only escape route from his world, a world thoroughly unconcerned with art. In his scrapbook, next to his own press clippings, he never failed to paste others dealing with the annual dinner of the Indépendants, including the most insignificant information about the salon. And to crown it all, he produced a celebration picture for the greater glory of the exhibitors. That is to say, for his own greater glory.

Rousseau in his studio, around 1907

As for the ordinary distinctive features which one might expect from the commonplace start of the sentence, they are to be found elsewhere. A first time, in his army registration slip of 1863: «Height: 5 ft. 6 inc. Face: oval. Forehead: round. Eyes: black. Nose: medium. Mouth: medium. Chin: round. Hair and eyebrows: dark brown. Distinguishing mark: cut on left ear.» And a second time, on the eve of his death: «Age: sixty-three, but looking between fifty and fifty-four. Medium height, about 5 ft. 6 inc. Build ordinary, hair dark brown, quite graying; whiskers rather thick but not too long, dark brown but also quite graying; face ordinary, complexion pale with a few reddish spots, eyes slightly sunk, walks with his head jutting forward, general appearance of a sickly man, deportment ordinary, hair now cut short but long in the past.»

Liberty Inviting the Artists to Exhibit at the 22nd Salon des Indépendants, 1906
Oil on canvas, 68⅞″ × 46½″ (175 × 118 cm). Kunsthaus, Zurich

Such was the man whom Apollinaire met around 1907. He kept in touch with him right up to his death in 1910. But did he really come to know him? Amid the Paris avant-garde Rousseau remained elusive. He did not mystify anyone nor was he mystified by anyone. It was only that, faced with this world which he felt to be alien and superior, he put up a front according to his lights in order to be on a par with the reception which he was given. He was something of a figure of fun but conscious of what set him apart from the others. The others were the young artists Picasso, Braque, Delaunay, and the poets around them; the Baroness d'Oettingen, alias Roch Grey, rich, idle and intelligent, who sincerely admired him; Vollard, the great dealer who bought his paintings. They are all people to whom Rousseau's friendship mattered less than theirs did to him. And for their sake he put on an act. The character whom he enacted for their benefit was often overloaded with naïveté because he was fully aware that there was no common measure between his problems and theirs. They did not speak the same language. Hence the considerable distortion of Rousseau's image in the memoirs of his contemporaries. The more precise their remembrances, the more limited they were to a single aspect of the Douanier which he had elected to display in front of them according to the circumstances and the beholder. And if the result was a pulverization and finally a betrayal of his personality, no one was to blame. Rousseau was splintered by his destiny. The character of the artist was incomprehensible to the simple people with whom he mingled in his district and who had not bothered to write down their memories, and Rousseau the ordinary man eluded the intellectuals who kept talking about him. No one really knew the whole of Rousseau. Nor did anybody even suspect a detail of his biography, made known only in 1953 following the discovery of some letters that had been preserved by sheer chance: he had been in serious trouble with the police over a case of forgery and use of forged documents, which had ended with his incarceration.

Rousseau in his studio

The most complete and precise information on Rousseau which we possess dates from a brief period of his life which he had never mentioned: his detention at the Santé Prison in December 1907 during the inquest on a case of fraud in which he had been mixed up. No sooner was Rousseau arrested than he began to write, addressing six long letters to the examining magistrate and one to his municipal counselor to make them aware of who he was. In these letters he retraced his entire life in an unceasing blend of facts and fancy. He tried to move the magistrate, exaggerated his merits, insisted that he was a great artist «favorably

THE SNAKE CHARMER, 1907. Oil on canvas, 65″ × 73¼″ (169 × 189.5 cm)
Louvre Museum, Paris

THE REPAST OF THE LION, 1907. Oil on canvas, 44¾″ × 63″ (113.5 × 160 cm)
The Metropolitan Museum of Art, New York. Bequest of Samuel A. Lewisohn

known in all the salon of Paris»; and, above all, having made a full confession, he asked to be let out of prison. A month later, on December 31, 1907, he was released on bail, but his case came to court after a year's delay, on January 9, 1909. According to the recollection of his defense attorney, one Guilhermet, he did not appear particularly intimidated on the stand. He seemed more saddened because all those present kept laughing at him. His attorney showed one of his paintings, an exotic landscape. Everybody burst out laughing. He showed his scrapbook and read some verses dedicated to Rousseau by an admiring lady. Renewed laughter. Then the painter Maximilien Luce testified in favor of Rousseau and praised his work. He was followed by the counsel for the defense; and he had no sooner ended his plea than Rousseau's voice was heard loud and clear: «Look here, now that you've said it all, can I go home?» The courtoom exploded in irrepressible laughter. The verdict was announced: Rousseau was fined a hundred francs and received a suspended sentence of two years' imprisonment. But the eminent lawyer Maurice Garçon, who unearthed Rousseau's letters from the dusty file where they had been forgotten, reached a startling conclusion: if the prosecution had dug out the sentence passed on Rousseau for petty theft committed when he was nineteen «he would quite simply have run the risk of being committed to hard labor.» This petty larceny was again something that Rousseau never mentioned. Perhaps he had even completely forgotten about it, his painting having wiped clean his past.

THE MERRY JESTERS, 1906. Oil on canvas, 57⅜″ × 44⅝″ (145.5 × 113.5 cm)
The Philadelphia Museum of Art. The Louise and Walter Arensberg Collection

Ten days before he was due to appear in court, on December 26, 1908, Rousseau wrote to Apollinaire: « I am still waiting for your charming Muse to sit for me at least once more. Otherwise everything is fine, I've found poet's carnations . . . »

He needed these poet's carnations for the final touches to the double portrait of Apollinaire with Marie Laurencin on which he had been working for several months. Their emblematic value is evident, but we shall never know with any degree of certainty what exact meaning had been ascribed to them to make them so important in the history of this painting. No doubt they are some sort of screen, but what are they screening?

To paint flowers, to arrange them in bouquets, had always been for Rousseau the simplest of gestures, the one that came most naturally to him, since the bouquet was a pretext for a chromatic unfolding unhampered by any problem of construction. Busy varying and combining his colors, he occasionally cared so little about nature that in 1909 he painted some bouquets in which tulips were crowned with fantastic corollas with alternate yellow and red petals. But now, for Apollinaire's portrait, he suddenly required the precise flowers which he had decided to put in the foreground, and on December 4, 1908, he wrote to the poet, either deliberately or inadvertently playing on the ambiguity of the French word « œillet » which means both « carnation » and « buttonhole »: « Don't you forget the flowers for the poets' (sic) buttonhole » which could perhaps be construed as meaning that certain flowers (possibly carnations) suit poets. And in the postscript to the same letter, he underlined the words: « Think above all of the flowers. » Finally he himself managed to find these flowers that had been a source of constant preoccupation. But he got them wrong, and instead of carnations he painted some ordinary gillyflowers. So, allegedly in order to correct this minor mistake, he hastened to produce a second portrait, theoretically an identical copy of the portrait with gillyflowers which he had unhesitatingly sent to the Salon des Indépendants. It is clear that the false emblem did not bother Rousseau. Then what did?

By sheer chance, Apollinaire published all the letters addressed to him by Rousseau while he was working on these two portraits. These letters make it possible to guess, to a certain extent, the attitude of the artist. On the one hand, this interminable chore entitled him to keep in constant touch with Apollinaire, whom he asked time and again to come and sit for him (which the poet never did). On the other hand, Apollinaire had not paid for his portrait. To make a copy was a smart way of bringing the picture back to his studio after the exhibition. Finally, in view of the celebrity of the sitter, Rousseau was anxious to keep this portrait for himself, and he retained the first version, by far the more polished, which he sold to Vollard. It would therefore appear that these poet's carnations were but a cover for pecuniary problems: they were both foreground and background to the scene where the real game was played: « I hope that you will be good enough to let me have an advance for my work on your portrait. I have been asked by a lot of people how much I had got for it; I have answered three hundred francs and they have all found that it was quite cheap; it is true that it is all between pals . . . I am in dire straits and all I have left tonight for my dinner are fifteen centimes » (April 28, 1909). « Today, all I have for my meals are a few centimes and there is nothing coming before next week. I have no idea what I will do. And I also have thirty-five francs to pay for a garment which I badly need because I don't have anything decent, and as you know I have to be out and about; my shoes are also cracking up. Just

THE MUSE INSPIRING
THE POET, 1909
Oil on canvas
51⅝″ × 38⅛″
(130 × 97 cm)
Pushkin Museum
of Fine Arts, Moscow

«I posed for the Douanier a number of times: first of all, he measured my nose, my mouth, my ears, my forehead, my hands, my whole body, and he conveyed these measurements onto the canvas exactly, reducing them to the size of the frame. During this time Rousseau used to sing me the songs of his childhood to entertain me, for posing is boring work.»

Apollinaire

THE MUSE INSPIRING
THE POET, 1909
Oil on canvas
57½" × 38⅛"
(146 × 97 cm)
Kunstmuseum, Basel

POET'S FLOWERS, 1890. Oil on canvas, 15″ × 18⅛″ (38 × 46 cm)
Collection: Mr. and Mrs. Paul Mellon, Upperville, Virginia

think that for over a year now I have been rather on the losing side» (July 1, 1909). And at the same time he wrote: «The whole background of the Muse is finished and so are the second and third planes; all that is left are the foreground and the figures» (July 8, 1909). «Things are getting difficult, because you did not come for the sitting and for certain tones I was in big trouble but managed nevertheless from memory» (August 3, 1909). Which were Rousseau's real worries?

Having made a mistake over the flowers and having made use of the mistake to ensure both Apollinaire's presence and payment for the portrait, did he not feel in danger of losing the one because of the other? Was there not beneath the slyness a real naïveté, and, mingled with both, true anguish? To decipher Rousseau's behavior is no easier than to reach the core of his painting. This world-famous portrait proves it: work on it progressed and did not progress amid a most curious correspondence, sprinkled with, among other things, brief notes in which Rousseau invited Apollinaire and his Muse to attend the «familial and friendly» parties which he gave in his studio.

FLOWERS, 1890–95. Oil on canvas, 24″ × 19½″ (61 × 49.5 cm). The Tate Gallery, London

Rousseau to Apollinaire:

Paris, November 10, 1909

Dear Friend,

Just a few words to remind you that tomorrow night Thursday the 11th of this month, the literary artistic gathering will meet, and we expect you and your Muse who will sing for us some gay and charming songs.

Meanwhile, a cordial handshake; till tomorrow night, eight thirty.

Your friend.

H. Rousseau

Paris, December 21, 1909

Dear Friend,

Just a few lines to let you know that tomorrow night, Thursday 23rd, I'm giving a familial, artistic party at which I hope to see you both and that you will kindly contribute as everybody wants you to.

Till tomorrow night, a cordial handshake; my best to our friends.

Your friend.

H. Rousseau

1re Partie

Orchestre.

1. H. Rousseau. Les deux frères. pas redoublé.
2. Mr Giriel. C'est un locataire.
3. Henri. L'Amour qui rit.
4. Mlle Jeanne. En me montrant des roses. Musique de Paulette Darty. Paroles de Maurice de Féraudy.
5. Mr Georgeus. Oublions le passé.
6. Mlle Paula Valmond. C'est le Vent.
7. Mr Charles. Conte Louis XV.
8. Rêverie de Schumann
   Mlle Hélène Freschas .... Piano
   Mr Maurice Parin .... Violon

2e Partie.

Orchestre.

1. H. Rousseau. Clémence. Valse.
2. Mr Renncler. Si l'on s'aime
3. Giriel. La Guillotine.
4. Henri. Tire Rinette.
5. Mlle Paula Valmond. Sur la Jetée. de Jacques Normand
6. Mr Charles. La Glu de Jean Richepin
7. Georgeus. Ola le temps qui tourne à l'orage.
8. Mlle Jeanne. Duo. Si j'ai ton coeur.
9. La Veuve Joyeuse. Frantz Léhar.
   Mlle Hélène Freschas .... Piano
   Mr Maurice Parin .... Violon

3e Partie

Duo de la Norma.

1. Mr Marchand .... Piano
   H. Rousseau .... Violon
2. Mr Charles. Les petites Barraques.
3. Mlle Jeanne. Les Serments sont folies
4. Tam-Tam Américain.
   Mr H. Rousseau, Mlle Jeannette
   Mr Marchand.
5. Mr Giriel. Garde le ma jolie.
6. Henri. La Poupée de Noël.
7. Georgeus. Mais elle est si jolie.
8. Mr H. Rousseau, Dans son répertoire.

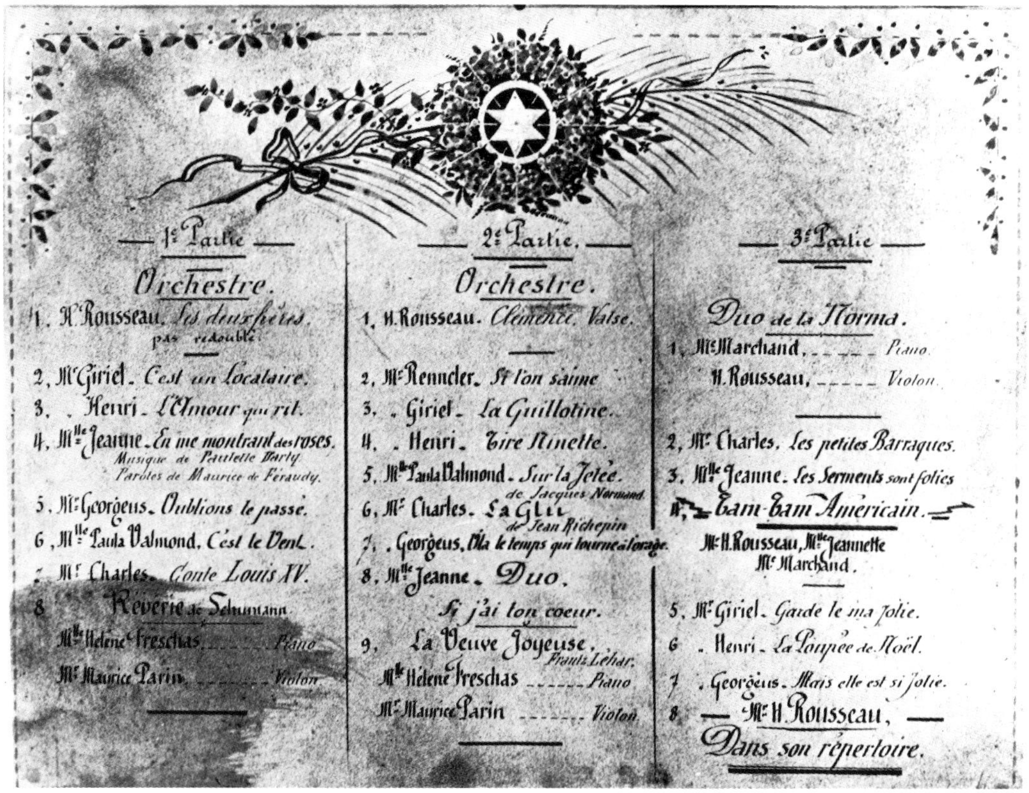

Rousseau, seated at the left, amidst his guests

Rousseau saw in his association with Apollinaire a corroboration of his own fame as an artist. And since this fame was still rather shaky, he transmuted it into certitude by displacing it a few removes to a level that appeared to be not unlike a reflection of reality.

Neither a dream nor true celebrity, he relished it at the parties which he gave in his studio from 1908 on. The relation between himself and the world that made fun of him was turned upside down. He was no longer the eccentric creature laughed at in his district, the poor simpleton. He was Monsieur Henri Rousseau, teacher at the Ecole Philotechnique, an artist well known in Paris, it was enough to see the guests at his parties. The baker's wife in her finery, the grocer, and the milkman could indeed meet at his place, depending on the day, Apollinaire or Picasso or Delaunay, Max Jacob, André Salmon, Georges Duhamel, Marie Laurencin, Braque, and foreigners too: the American artist Max Weber, the German art critics Wilhelm Uhde, Adolphe Basler . . . Unimaginable parties for which Rousseau would design the programs, have them stenciled in red and purple, and send them to his friends.

This touching parody of high society manners sometimes ended with a sentence indicating Rousseau's zeal: « The Stage is at the disposal of all guests. » On another program, as an accomplished host, he « craved the kind participation of his guests. » And, being a good republican, he never forgot the « Marseillaise. » Finally, to an invitation of July 1909, he added: « Please inform your friends. » The doors of his studio were wide open to all his admirers, known and unknown. Monsieur Henri Rousseau entertained.

Dog Lying on Cushion, 1890–95. Oil on wood, 8⅞″ × 10⅞″ (22.5 × 27.5 cm)
Private collection

PÈRE JUNIET'S CART, 1908. Oil on canvas, 38⅛″ × 50¾″ (97 × 129 cm)
Louvre Museum, Paris

PORTRAIT OF A WOMAN, 1895. Oil on canvas, 59″ × 39⅜″ (150 × 100 cm)
Louvre Museum, Paris. Collection Pablo Picasso

Henri Rousseau entertained and was entertained.

In 1908 Picasso had found a large *Portrait of a Woman* by Rousseau in a junk-shop and had bought it for five francs. (At that time he was selling his own drawings to the same dealer at a franc per piece.) To celebrate the event, he decided to organize a banquet in honor of Rousseau in his studio at the Bateau-Lavoir. Fernande Olivier, who was his constant companion in those days, Maurice Reynal, and Gertrude Stein have left us descriptions of the scene. Though their recollections do not entirely tally, the mood which they evoke is the same and makes the banquet look like a full-bodied version of the life-style in Paris at the turn of the century, the fabulous Belle Epoque.

The guests took their places at a trestle table; garlands of Chinese lanterns shimmered in the studio. Rousseau's painting hung on the wall, and floating across a profusion of flags, a large streamer read: «Honor to Rousseau.»

«Amidst the general uproar, three gentle knocks at the door cut all the noise dead. In the complete silence, the door opened; it was the Douanier, wearing his floppy felt hat and carrying in his left hand his cane and in his right his violin. . . . This was certainly one of the most moving pictures by Rousseau. He took a look around the room, the lanterns enchanted him, his face lit up.»

Now the banquet could begin. But the food, ordered from some caterer, never seemed to arrive. The guests had been waiting for two hours when Picasso suddenly realized that he had given the wrong date when ordering the meal. It was then that the party really took off. «As the host had some fifty bottles of some standing, things were soon put right. Songs and speeches began to flow. Rousseau got hold of his violin and played "Clémence," the waltz which he had written. Apollinaire improvised a long poem in praise of Rousseau.»

O peintre glorieux de l'alme République,
Ton nom est le drapeau des fiers Indépendants
Et dans le marbre blanc, issu du Pentélique,
On sculptera ta face, orgueil de notre temps.

Glorious painter of our dear Republic
Your name is the flag of the proud Indépendants
And it is in white marble wrested from the Pentelic
That your features will be sculptured, pride of our age.

The suggestion has been made that it was all a big farce. But even if it were so for some, Rousseau, proudly seated on his «throne made of a chair poised on a packing case,» which Picasso had rigged for him on the spot, was living through his hour of consecration. Later, when the company was growing more and more restless around him, he dozed off in his seat.

Photograph of «The Dream» from Rousseau's personal papers

Apollinaire in the «Intransigeant» of March 18, 1910: «That the painting emanates beauty is incontestable . . . I think that this year no one will dare to laugh . . . Ask painters what they think. They are unanimous: they all admire it. They admire everything about it, even the Louis-Philippe settee swallowed up in the virgin forest, and they are right.»

This is the title of Rousseau's last painting. And no title could better convey at all levels the significance of this picture which seems to raise to the highest degree the power and the achievement of Rousseau as well as the gulf between what he did and what he thought he was doing. On one side, his intentions; on the other, their outcome, without anything to bridge them.

On one side, this letter to the art critic André Dupont:

> Dear Sir,
>
> I hasten to reply to your kind letter and to let you know why the settee in question is there. The woman asleep on the settee dreams that she has been moved to this forest, hearing the charmer's instrument. This gives you the reason why this settee is in the picture . . .

On the other, this confession to Arsène Alexandre:

> I don't know if you are like me, but when I go into these hothouses and I see these strange plants from exotic lands, it seems to me that I am entering a dream. I feel myself quite a different man . . .

This different man was now holding the brush. Rousseau daydreamed just like the woman lying on the red settee. He had swung to the other side where the unconscious alone was at work. Without constraint and without a model, served by a long experience of painting, his hand built up a compact space ordered in a rhythm scanned by the spiky vegetation. Arsène Alexandre had seen Rousseau at work: « I cast a glance . . . at his palette, which he was using at that moment to obtain the greens of his exotic forest, for he works on all the identical tones in a picture at the same time and I have never seen a palette gleam with so many greens. » Ardengo Soffici, himself a painter, was even more startled by Rousseau's working habits: he had penciled all the outlines of the tropical vegetation while only here and there covering some portions with different shades of green. Rousseau, who was keeping count of the greens while putting them on any odd spot of the picture, informed him that he was on his twenty-second green. He was brushing on the same tone again and again, carefully cleaning his palette at each changeover.

A strange technique, which Rousseau used for the first time in his exotic landscapes. Always prone to multiply the colors in a landscape, he now found in such chromatic wealth the very principle of his works and applied it in all lucidity. He faced up squarely to the language of painting, which he articulated without any more aiming at any resemblance. All by himself and in his own way, he bypassed the problem of imitation which was then the most topical. He was therefore fully entitled to show at the salon of the new avant-garde, the Salon d'Automne, where he exhibited as early as 1905. What is most astonishing is to see how this sixty-year-old autodidact fell into step with the young: his *Hungry Lion* was hung in the central room of all places, beside paintings by Matisse, Derain, Vlaminck, those

THE DREAM, 1910. Oil on canvas, 80½″ × 117½″ (204.5 × 299 cm)
The Museum of Modern Art, New York. Gift of Nelson A. Rockefeller

This painting was exhibited
at the Salon d'Automne in 1910,
with the following caption:

Yadwigha dans un beau rêve
S'étant endormie doucement
Entendait les sons d'une musette
Dont jouait un charmeur bien pensant
Pendant que la lune reflète
Sur les fleurs, les arbres verdoyants
Les fauves serpents prêtent l'oreille
Aux airs gais de l'instrument.

(Yadwigha, peacefully asleep,
Enjoys a lovely dream:
She hears a kind snake charmer
Playing upon his reed.
On stream and foliage glisten
The silvery beams of the moon;
And savage serpents listen
To the gay, entrancing tune.)

who, that very year, would be nicknamed the « Fauves. » And who knows if his vast virgin forest with its real wild beast did not conjure up, by a natural association of ideas, this label, which was purely symbolic with regard to those whom it was meant to criticize. The press was full of praise for his picture. Even the conservative « Illustration » reproduced it on its double spread devoted to the Salon d'Automne.

Rousseau thus entered the last period of his life, culminating in *The Dream*. From his past, he preserved the need to follow a model and sometimes traced with the pantograph the outlines of the wild animals seen in his exotic landscapes. However, the theme which he proceeded to develop with ever-increasing freedom was vegetation, exuberantly spreading its intertwined pattern all over the pictures, which were now, without exception, rather large. This vegetation has been termed tropical. Its density and its tangle surely warrant the label. For this reason it has been linked to Rousseau's alleged journey to Mexico or to the hothouses of the Paris Botanical Gardens. The attempt has thus been made, in one way or another, to presuppose an external model for these plants, while in fact they stem from the interior, from the very development of Rousseau's pictorial idiom. The intertwining and density of these forms conceived on a tropical model ultimately solved a problem that had plagued Rousseau: space. This had been a stubborn stumbling block for him, as he had never managed to bow to conventional perspective. To set a succession of planes, to construct a three-dimensional space, and to suggest its depth had always been beyond his means. Now, by virtue of the disposition and repartition of these inextricable forms, which he varied at will without any conventional spatial constraint, he could at long last create a full space very clearly stated in chromatic terms. The true exuberance of the vegetation was there in the color. As for the plants themselves, they were made up of unidentifiable patterns that might just as well have been found in the most widely known European flora. But they had been altered beyond recognition: alienated from real space, nullified by their own configurations, they are, by the same token, endowed with a much greater power of persuasion. The exotic appearance which emerges from this transmutation was but the apparition of the enigmatic power of imagination swelling from the deepest recesses of creativity. Again Rousseau said this in his own way, a few months before his death, when he painted *The Dream*.

*

*　　　*

EXOTIC LANDSCAPE, 1910. Oil on canvas, 51¼″ × 64″ (130.2 × 162.5 cm)
The Norton Simon Foundation, Los Angeles

89

THE JUNGLE: TIGER ATTACKING A BUFFALO, 1908. Oil on canvas, 67¾″ × 75⅜″ (172 × 191.5 cm) The Cleveland Museum of Art. Gift of Hanna Fund

NEGRO ATTAQUED BY A JAGUAR, 1910. Oil on canvas, 44⅛″ × 66⅛″ (114 × 162 cm). Kunstmuseum, Basel

THE HUNGRY LION, 1905. Oil on canvas, 78¾″ × 120″ (200 × 300 cm). Private collection

Rousseau died in September 1910. On his tombstone, Brancusi and the painter Ortiz de Zarate engraved the following epitaph, which Apollinaire had written in pencil:

> Gentil Rousseau tu nous entends
> Nous te saluons
> Delaunay sa femme Monsieur Queval et moi
> Laisse passer nos bagages en franchise à la porte du ciel
> Nous t'apporterons des pinceaux, des couleurs, des toiles
> Afin que tes loisirs sacrés dans la lumière réelle
> Tu les consacres à peindre comme tu tiras mon portrait
> La face des étoiles.

> (Gentle Rousseau you can hear us
> We salute you
> Delaunay his wife Monsieur Queval and myself
> Let our luggage pass duty-free through the gate of heaven
> We are bringing you brushes paints and canvas
> That you may spend your sacred leisure hours
> Painting in the light of truth eternal
> As you once painted my portrait
> Facing the stars.)

ILLUSTRATIONS

Bibliographical references

The reader will find the detailed bibliographical references of all documents listed in the « Catalogue raisonné of the works of Henri Rousseau » published by Rizzoli, Milano in 1971 and in the monograph on Rousseau published in 1962 by Harry N. Abrams, New York. Translations of quotations were also taken from the Abrams monograph.

PHOTOGRAPHS

DuMont Buchverlag, Cologne – Editions du Cercle d'Art, Paris – Jacqueline Hyde, Paris – Lauros-Giraudon, Paris – André Morain, Paris – Rosie Rey – Service de Documentation Photographique de la Réunion des Musées Nationaux, Paris – Hans Hinz SWB, Allschwill, Switzerland – Dieter Widmer, Basel – André Held, Lausanne – Hauser und Woltensberger, Winterthur – Walter Dräyer, Zurich – John Webb, London – Robert E. Mates and Paul Katz, New York – Otto E. Nelson, New York.

We wish to thank the owners of the works by Henry Rousseau reproduced in this book:

MUSEUMS

CZECHOSLOVAKIA:
Narodni Galeri, Prague.

FRANCE:
Musée Carnavalet, Paris – Louvre Museum, Paris – Musée Massey, Tarbes.

SWITZERLAND:
Kunstmuseum, Basel – Kunstverein, Winterthur – Kunsthaus, Zurich.

U.K.
Courtauld Institute, London – National Gallery, London – Tate Gallery, London.

U.S.S.R.
Pushkin Museum, Moscow.

U.S.A.
Fogg Art Museum, Harvard University, Cambridge, Massachusetts – The Art Institute of Chicago – Cleveland Museum of Art – The Detroit Institute of Arts – Norton Simon Foundation, Los Angeles – Metropolitan Museum of Art, New York – Museum of Modern Art, New York – The Solomon R. Guggenheim Museum, New York – Philadelphia Museum of Art – Museum of Art, Carnegie Institute, Pittsburgh – National Gallery of Art, Washington, D.C.

PRIVATE COLLECTIONS

Michael Bakwin – Nina Kandinsky, Neuilly-sur-Seine, France – Mr. and Mrs. Paul Mellon, Upperville, Virginia – Christophe Tzara, Sceaux, France.